LET'S FIND OUT ABOUT **NEIGHBORS**

FRANKLIN WATTS, INC.
575 Lexington Avenue, New York, N.Y. 10022

LET'S FIND OUT ABOUT
NEIGHBORS

BY VALERIE PITT   PICTURES BY PAMELA BALDWIN-FORD

SBN 531-00058-3

1 2 3 4 5 6

LET'S FIND OUT ABOUT **NEIGHBORS**

Your neighbor is someone who lives near
  you.
Everyone is a neighbor to someone else.

Your neighbors live all around you—in
your building, next door, and in the few
blocks around your home.

You depend on your neighbors for
　friendship.
You go to school with your neighbors.

You play with your neighbors.

You rely on your neighbors for help, too.
When you go away on vacation, your
neighbors might help you by taking in
your mail, or feeding your pet.

If your neighbor is ill your mother might
help her by doing some of her shopping
or taking care of her children.

The very best neighbors are those who
   are neighborly.
Neighborly people are friendly and helpful
   to their neighbors.

Good neighbors can be like having an
extra family around you.

All neighbors are different.

Your neighbors may be old or young.

They may be black or white.

They may have big families for you to play
   with.
They may live alone.
What are your neighbors like?

Together with your neighbors, you and
    your family live in a neighborhood.
A neighborhood is a small group of streets
    and houses close by each other.
Your neighborhood is the few blocks
    around your home where you play and
    shop and perhaps go to school.

There are all kinds of neighborhoods.
A village is a small group of houses, shops,
    and people.

Because it is so small, the whole village is
really one neighborhood and all the
people are neighbors.

If you live in a village you may get to know
    everyone.
Already you may know the mailman and
    the doctor and the butcher and the
    bus driver.
You know the children in your class at
    school.

And you know most of the neighborhood
dogs and cats.
A village is a friendly place because
everyone lives and works near each
other.

Maybe you live in a suburb.
A suburb is an area just outside a city, full
of houses and apartments.

People live in a suburb and go into the
city to work and shop.

Because it is bigger than a village, a
   suburb has many neighborhoods.
But all the neighborhoods are very much
   alike.
Can you see why?

It is because all suburbs have mostly
houses and very few shops.

If you live in a suburb you will meet many
of the children in your own neighborhood.
You will go to the same school and play
in the same park.

Because there are not many neighborhood
   shops, your mother may drive to a
   shopping center.
A shopping center is a large group of
   shops built next to each other.

Sometimes all the shops are under one roof.
This is called a shopping mall.
Here your mother can do all her shopping
at one time and in one place.

Perhaps you live in a big city, like New York or Chicago.

Big cities have lots and lots of different
   neighborhoods.
Many neighborhoods joined together make
   one huge city.

If you live in a big city and your school is
   in another neighborhood, you may have
   to take a bus to get there.

You may have to take a bus or subway to
get to the big shopping areas, too.

Around your neighborhood you will find
small shops where you can buy most of
the things you need.
There will probably be a grocery store, a
drugstore, and a laundromat.

If your neighborhood is quite large, there
will be a supermarket, a bank, and
maybe a movie, too.

Some neighborhoods in big cities are
 made up of people from other countries.
Perhaps your parents are from Italy and
 you live in an Italian neighborhood.
The corner grocer will have lots of
 sausages and salamis hanging from the
 ceiling.
You will see long fresh loaves of bread
 and all kinds of pasta—spaghetti and
 macaroni and many others.
The neighbors around you will be
 speaking Italian.
It will be like living half in Italy and half in
 America.

Just as you depend on your neighbors, so
the shops in your neighborhood depend
on the people who live nearby.

The butcher depends on people in the
neighborhood to buy his meat.
With the money he gets from selling his
meat he can buy things for his family.

By buying things and spending money in
the neighborhood, everyone helps to
keep it alive and growing.

People are not the only ones who have
neighbors.

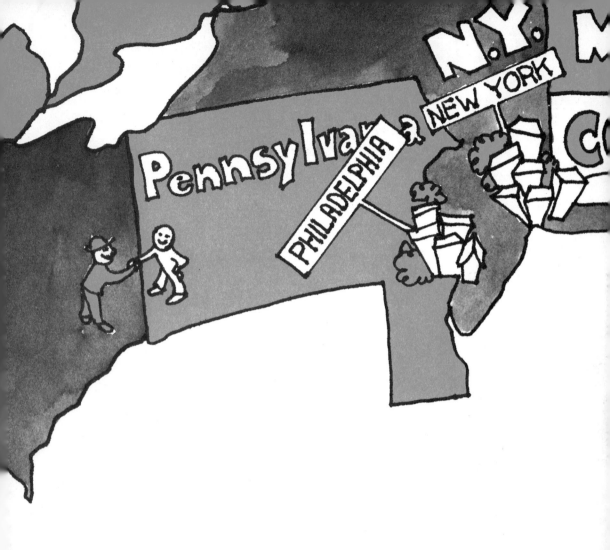

Because "neighboring" means "nearby,"
villages and cities and states have
neighbors, too.

The city nearest to the city you live in is a
neighboring city.

The states around your state are called
neighboring states.

CANA

UNITED

mexico

46

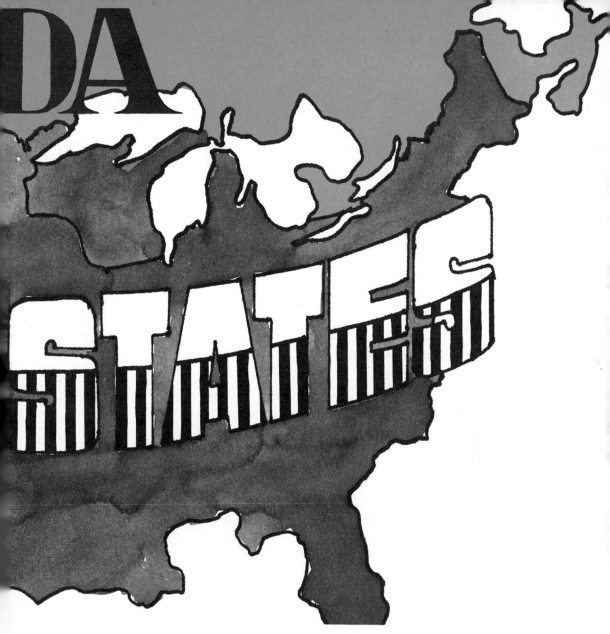

Even countries have neighbors, too.
The United States has two close
     neighboring countries.
It has Canada in the north and Mexico in
     the south.

Just as neighbors try to be helpful to each
    other, so do countries.
When they succeed it makes the whole
    world a friendly place.